WHEN I WAS STRAIGHT

A Tribute to Maureen Seaton

Edited by Dustin Brookshire

Harbor Editions
Small Harbor Publishing

Emma

Aaron

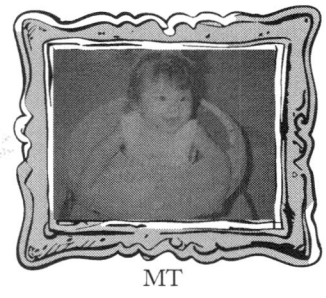
MT

When I Was Straight

Allison

Sarah

Travis

Diamond

Mel

Regie

Lesléa

J.D.

Nicole

When I Was Straight: A Tribute to Maureen Seaton
Copyright © 2024 by Dustin Brookshire
All rights reserved.

Cover photo by Emily Blank
Cover design by Kristiane Weeks-Rogers
Book layout by Claire Eder
Project Coordinated by Dustin Brookshire

WHEN I WAS STRAIGHT: A TRIBUTE TO MAUREEN SEATON
DUSTIN BROOKSHIRE
ISBN 978-1-957248-43-1
Harbor Anthologies,
an imprint of Small Harbor Publishing

Contents

Introduction	7
Foreword	9
Maureen Seaton	13
Kelli Russell Agodon	17
Clayre Benzadón	18
Allison Blevins	20
Emma Bolden	21
Dustin Brookshire	23
Regie Cabico	25
Sarah Cooper	26
James Davis	27
Theresa Davis	29
Aaron DeLee	31
Diamond Forde	32
Tyler Gillespie	33
J.D. Isip	34
Charles Jensen	35
Ben Kline	36
Travis Chi Wing Lau	37
Caridad Moro-Gronlier	38
Lesléa Newman	40
Mel Sherrer	43

Nicole Tallman	44
Addie Tsai	45
MT Vallarta	47
Julie Marie Wade	48
Afterword	51
The Extraordinary Maureen Seaton	55
Acknowledgements	59
Bios	61
About the Editor	67
About Small Harbor Publishing	69

Introduction

I fell in love with Maureen Seaton's work when she read at Java Monkey Speaks in the fall of 2004. I was taking poetry classes as electives at Georgia State University, and Maureen was the first rockstar poet that I had met. I can still close my eyes and see Maureen on the Java Monkey stage and hear her reading her poem "Furious Cooking." I sat in the audience in awe of Maureen. I've remained in awe of her since that day, and I'll remain in awe of everything she accomplished and who she was until the day I die. If you also knew Maureen, then you're nodding your head in agreement because you know exactly what I mean.

Maureen was kind enough to respond to my emails after that 2004 encounter and a friendship was born. She was a light. She was kind. She was funny. She was generous. Maureen was so very generous to people and especially poets. One of Maureen's superpowers was to make everyone she interacted with feel like the most special person on the planet.

On February 1, 2023, Denise Duhamel spotlighted Maureen Seaton's "When I Was Straight" and Julie Marie Wade's "When I Straight" in the *Best American Poetry Blog*. I hadn't thought about Maureen's "When I Was Straight" in a long time, but reading the poem in the *BAP Blog* brought me the same joy I experienced the first time I read it. (That's the sign of a hell of a poem!) I had to revisit Maureen's *Little Ice Age* (Invisible City Press, 2001). Maureen has a few "When I Was…" poems in the collection, and I appreciate them all. "When I Was Straight" wouldn't leave my thoughts. I had to write my own "When I Was Straight." I shared my poem with Maureen with a thank you for inspiring me, and she was gracious in her response.

I also couldn't stop asking myself. What stories would other LGBTQIA+ poets tell if they wrote a poem titled "When I Was Straight?" In March 2023, I started inviting poets to read Maureen's poem and write their own. The only steadfast rule was that poets had to title their poem "When I Was Straight." Now, here we are with 23 poets sharing their "When I Was Straight" poems.

I'm sad that I can't share this book with Maureen. We lost the gift that is Maureen Seaton on August 26, 2023. This book is my way of honoring my friend.

In 2023, thanks to the leadership of the *South Florida Poetry Journal*, with support from *Limp Wrist*, we launched The Maureen Seaton Poetry Prize. (I can't stress enough that this contest is only possible thanks to my friends at *SoFloPoJo*!) The editor royalties from this book will support the prize.

Thank you for spending time with these poems and honoring Maureen's legacy.

Dustin Brookshire
April 5, 2024
When I Was Straight: A Tribute to Maureen Seaton Editor

Foreword

Maureen was a beloved teacher at the University of Miami and in many community workshop settings, including Reading Queer. Her pedagogy was gentle, inspiring, and supportive. Yet, perhaps, what we can learn most from her is via the very poems themselves. Maureen's "When I Was Straight" was one of those instant classics. It was a poem that I'd call many a friend to read over the phone (pre-social media days). "When I Was Straight" was featured on *Verse Daily* shortly after *Little Ice Age* was published. It is written in terza rima, a form known for its echoes and anticipation. Maureen filled the poem with intricate and funny slant rhymes—such as nipples, fickle, and fragile. The whole poem told it "slant," as Emily Dickenson would say. It's a coming out poem—true—but also a "looking back" poem, full of compassion and the foreshadowing of Maureen's later life of openness, exploration, and freedom.

Dustin Brookshire has gathered an impressive array of poetic emulations in *When I Was Straight: A Tribute to Maureen Seaton*. They include free verse gestures, couplets, tercets, and prose poems. Maureen's influence shines, though is never blinding—each of the poets in this anthology takes her title and makes the poem that follows their own. James Davis has a blast with exact rhymes and slant rhymes in his quatrains—drunk/humped, stoner/boner, Soloflex/impressed. And peppered throughout the poets' work, you'll find delightful plays on the word "straight" that reverberate from Maureen's "straightforward sessions in bed" and "(s)traight as gin." Clayre Benzadón's "Straight / // edged." Dustin Brookshire's "I'd sit back straight . . ." Theresa Davis declaring, "I was SAT PREP strategy/ straight/ all through high school . . ." Caridad Moro-Gronlier pushes such wordplay to the tenderly hilarious extreme—with "straight man," "straight-faced," "straight arrow," "straight flush," "straight shooter," "(s)traightaway," "straight-laced," "straitjacket," "straight edged razor," "straight up," "straightforward," and "just how dire the straits . . ." until she leaves a marriage to a man by walking "straight out the door."

Many of the poems in this anthology explore early awakenings to desire. Kelli Russell Agodon writes:

> . . .how I always wanted
>
> to be Tom Sawyer, somewhat for the raft,
> somehow to be closer to the perfect
>
> Becky Thatcher . . .

Three poems point to the thrilling and treacherous space of sleepovers. Allison Blevins talks of the experience of a teenage girl, "Silent in her bed, her fingers touched my arm—gentle as blue and sweet corn and pond water lapping." At another sleepover, Diamond Forde tells us "the birthday girl was Britney & each time their hands fluttered like dizzy birds to meet, I swallowed honey, spoke a quiet sweet enough to drown." And Julie Marie Wade writes:

> When I stood up, I tried to tiptoe
> around the sleeping bodies, their long hair
> speckled with confetti, their faces blanched by the
> porch-light moon.

Others look back on early lust and the dangerous pleasure of looking. Reggie Cabico tells us, "I crushed on Mr. Rink, the choir leader,/who was so hot nuns swooned as he sauntered /past lockers in his tight white shorts . . ." Aaron DeLee masturbates in a shower—"I had seven minutes to fix my stare/on *The Gentle Rogue*'s pectoral muscles. . . ." Lesléa Newman's poem describes a teenager watching other girls putting on lipstick in the bathroom:

> . . .one of them glared
> back and asked, "What are you, a lezzie?"
> which made all the others shriek
> with laughter. . . .

Poets explore not only the shame they feel from their peers, but also from their parents. Nicole Tallman writes, "I hung onto hope like my mother,/who said she'd rather I had cancer/than be *that way*." Dustin Brookshire's poem ends:

> . . .my father would say,
> *I'd rather one of my sons*
> *blow my brains out*
> *than tell me he's gay.*

Maureen's poem enacts the performance of straight sex: you could count on me for bold orgasms, for/trapeze art and graceful aerobics, oh/ there is no lover like a panicked lover. Poets included in this anthology write moving counterparts of the trappings of heterosexual couplings, especially fertility and a possible unwanted child. Ben Kline's prose poem imagines what his life might have been if his girlfriend Andi had gotten pregnant and they couldn't afford an abortion—". . .any kid / would be turning 30 now / Fuck / I'd be a grandpa / probably Pawpaw / married at last / to a man / maybe two . . ." Sarah Cooper's poem begins:

> other straight people told me my body had purpose.
>   They promised my body could make another body,
>   that my body would carry a being waiting to be.

How did they not know how terrifying that sounds
    to a child? . . .

She deftly turns to the natural world "muddy holes" where she finds tadpoles.
    It's astounding to me the twists and turns the poems make in this impressive volume, insuring Maureen's legacy. Happy reading!

Denise Duhamel
April 6, 2024
Hollywood, FL

Maureen Seaton

When I Was Straight

When I was straight I dreamed of nipples,
my dreams were crowded with cleavage and yin,
I read a book that said if you are fickle

about sex, note your obsession in dreams
then do the opposite in real life. This
made sense, my boyfriend said, although it seemed

oddly like a game of Exquisite Corpse
to me. We'd make love, I'd dream of figs,
that drizzled pink, and sometimes I'd lapse

into madrigals (meaning: of the womb), big
leap from the straightforward sessions in bed
of linearity and menthol. Legs

would cross and uncross in my dreams, heads
fall back with me at the throat. I adored
the winged clavicle, that link between breast-

bone and scapula. Straight as gin, I poured
myself into pretense and fellatio,
you could count on me for bold orgasms, for

trapeze art and graceful aerobics, oh
there is no lover like a panicked lover.
Once I dreamed of abandoning the Old

Boyfriend Theory of Headache and Blunder-
buss. Believe me, I said, this will hurt him
more than me, but the dream laughed! Torture

me, I thought, now that even my id
has turned against me, there is something fragile
here to lose, exquisite truth, and I did.

. . . My heart throws itself to the stars.
To see which ones decide to stand still

And grow a constellation around me.

Maureen Seaton, "Save Yourself for Better Times"

Kelli Russell Agodon

When I Was Straight

I thought everyone was easy
to love. The boys who brought me

bouquets of daisies and the girls
who braided my hair at slumber

parties, the girls I didn't dare to tell.
When I was straight, I was mostly curved,

a windy road of fading madronas, a sunset
on a dead-end street holding the Indigo

Girls in one hand and Elvis Costello
in the other. Remember how I always wanted

to be Tom Sawyer, somewhat for the raft,
somehow to be closer to the perfect

Becky Thatcher. Looking back it seems easy
to understand how I was in love

with all the world, how every exit was also
a possibility. *Everyone is easy to love,*

is what the meadow tells me in wild-
flowers—a daisychain woven into my braids.

Clayre Benzadón

When I Was Straight

A high school boyfriend read
a poem in front of a crowd
to ask me to prom, he insisted

he wanted to get married.
With a fear. No, not him: I was the one a-
    fraid (fraud). Straight /

edged. I thought *there can only
be one way to love*, so the path
was to find a boyfriend, then

get hitched. Then I switched.
In college, my whole head would turn
red, my chest would beat

as I stared too long at the woman
with the dyed hair and piercings
walking adjacent from me

to the same poetry class,
and I adhered, I had to hear myself
say to myself, *you just like her*

style. But I knew deep inside
me my body was urging,
wildly hot, and wet.

I was straight, I told myself
until I leaned in, took her
in like desire was an end-

less vessel, I was moving
my mouth all over her, messy
and crooked, deviant, and devil.

I never stopped (looked back).

Allison Blevins

When I Was Straight

When I was straight, my body was detached. My face, a portrait in every mirror, changed each night, some new arrangement of drip and swirl, watercolor hair, my lips thin pastel rose then absurdly large and quirked at each corner. My body now still resists recognition, insists on new arrangements of color and sound. But when I was straight, my eyes sang most mornings, sang a language of green and gold—something felt promised to me then, at 13, at 15, so young, fresh mourning in my mouth and breath, even behind closed doors, even afraid, even flat and still in my best friend's bed, our fingertips only just so, our hips pulling and pulling. Silent in her bed, her fingers touched my arm—gentle as blue and sweet corn and pond water lapping. Nothing would ever be the same after—that pain promised—how want burned, want wetted our lips and teeth. In Japan, they have a word for when your mouth is lonely. Pain promised to never let go at 16 in her bed, on our backs, our barely touching skin. When I was straight, I hoped that pain might last forever.

Emma Bolden

When I Was Straight

In Catholic School we kneeled to learn
what it meant to be holy. On the playground
our classmates taught a different catechism

about what happened on your knees, how
a girl could lead a boy to ascension, a heaven
kingdomed within the bedrooms of our world.

It's only natural, they preached, the girls
with older sisters, older cousins, mothers
with lips loosened by their nightly sacrament

of Chardonnay. From the mount of grass
by the tire swings they sermoned sex as a gift
from God, sacred like a prayer. I couldn't

understand. I couldn't divine within my nature
what Amanda, Leia, Lauren said—and I
believed, I believed—made us human:

the wet and the open and thrust, the flush
pinkslipping two cheeks curved towards
a body, another body. Nothing in me knew

what it meant to want. In mass, by my bed,
hidden behind the bathroom's lock I dropped
to my knees and prayed *O Lord make me*

normal, make me enough. I didn't know then
that there were other truths just as natural
within the body, about the body, I didn't yet know

that absence doesn't always mean you're lacking,
that being is being, is beautiful, and enough.

Dustin Brookshire

When I Was Straight

I stayed home
while my mother
drove to the grocery store.
Two hours alone to prance
in my mother's high heels,
wear her dresses and nightgowns,
and a white t-shirt as a wig.
I'd probe her jewelry box,
slip on a ring or two,
a necklace, and the bracelet
she only wore for special occasions.
I applied her lipstick with a smile.
I'd sit back straight, legs crossed
directing the household staff
that we didn't have
on the tasks of the day:
vacuum, mop, polish the china,
and press the laundry—
a boss lady before
being a boss lady was a thing.
I'd twirl around the living room
with one hand extended,
an invitation to a man
who wouldn't enter my life
for another thirty-five years.

When I was straight,
my father would say,
*I'd rather one of my sons
blow my brains out
than tell me he's gay.*

Regie Cabico

When I Was Straight

I crushed on Mr. Rink, the choir leader,
who was so hot nuns swooned as he sauntered
past lockers in his tight white shorts, occasionally
tussling my hair with his leather-scented hand.
He kept me after school almost every day
to rehearse my tenor lead in One Bread, One Body.
I dared not stare in his deep chocolate eyes.
When I harmonized with his baritone. I fought
the urge to reach down and touch his golden calves
glistening in the shaft of sunlight that penetrated
the stained-glass body of St. Michael. Queer desire
swelled but I stuffed the flutters of the Holy Ghost,
an obsidian rock inside me. All the straight girls
and closeted boys hated me but I wore my dutiful
halo, I stood on the altar like a solitary bowling pin
among hallowed penguins. Open-mouthed,
I warbled a high G as the glorious mysteries
bulged under my cassock.

Sarah Cooper

When I Was Straight

other straight people told me my body had purpose.
        They promised my body could make another body,
                that my body would carry a being waiting to be.

How did they not know how terrifying that sounds
        to a child? When I was straight someone I loved
                told me I wasn't & I didn't understand what that meant

except that I was different and that was wrong
        & that difference was a separation, a divide between me
                and the people I loved. So I tried to understand

what my differences were & I took a knife's tip
        dug them from me. I deposited
                my differences in shallow graves in a riverbed.

I prayed for heavy rains to wash them downstream
        to some other body who could embody being not straight.
                Years later when I tried to excavate them

I found muddy holes in the shore where
        a frog had laid her eggs and tadpoles swam
                in my emptied not-straightness. They thrived there.

James Davis

When I Was Straight

I was piss drunk,
a sophomore.
I flopped and humped
a basement floor

and swore I'd "fuck
a hundred hos."
My rainbow socks
with all ten toes

said otherwise.
I had to laugh
with the other guys
at my stagecraft.

I understudied
the part of Stoner
beneath some buddies
and a furtive boner.

We played *The Wall*
on a PlayStation
and gaped, enthralled
by the visualizations,

the way they matched
each song's *esprit*.
In short, I crashed.
I earned a C,

my very first,
in Honors Chem.
I grunted and cursed
in a muggy gym,

on the Soloflex.
My preacher curls
almost impressed
a Mormon girl.

To tell the truth,
it was kind of fun,
to act uncouth
and be no one,

to benefit
from politesse
that thinks you're straight
when you're a mess.

Theresa Davis

When I Was Straight

Of dubious authenticity
an origin story
of my own divining
I was SAT PREP strategy
straight
all through high school

arcane thoughts of traditional
never clung to the taste of my skin
if it was pleasure I sought
It could surely be found
science fair special
football
or
pom-poms

maybe it was the easy
in their desperation
that drew me to them
the ability to bend,
the quick in and out of ideas
soon forgotten

maybe it was the easy
of conversation

to the tune of dry humping
that made me linger
in soft places
I probably should have figured it out
maybe I did

by college the thought of vacillating
between the two
no longer appealed to me
not willing to name a thing

I took to learning body language
in a different direction
my path more meander
than rush hour
still
moving in the same direction
just replacing straight
with
forward

Aaron DeLee

When I Was Straight

       I had seven minutes to fix my stare
on *The Gentle Rogue*'s pectoral muscles
       shining bright as a full moon, while water
pummeled the tub's basin, inching upward,
       and imagine myself as that red-headed
damsel backing her ass into his black
       leather chaps; seven minutes to tug *Savage
Thunder*'s tanned vest and bury my face
       in his firm, smooth chest while stallions
ran wild across the sun-kissed badlands
       surrounding us; steam fogged the mirror
within seven minutes and then it was drawn,
       the bath, echoing any stray final drips
onto its stillness, and my fricative
       rubbing and heavy panting could be heard
through our home's papery walls, I was sure.
       It was a race to finish; and to come out
looking innocent was a fantasy.

Diamond Forde

When I Was Straight

The van mumbled in rush hour, a cemetery yawning gray teeth across the hillside to our right. "Hold your breath," the birthday girl said, & all five girls 'cept me clap shut, hands smacking their happy mouths, matching bracelets nibbling red marks in their cheeks

& it wasn't because I couldn't afford a bracelet. & it wasn't because this was my first sleepover (though it was, twelve & never spent a night not home)

or that when I entered the birthday girl's home I stumbled on stairs that went forever, stiffened hallways, a white couch, a stand mixer, one lilac room all hers—the birthday girl—who made us play celebrities, so I stilted into Ashanti (because her songs carried me through all my imagined heartaches—the first, that none of you knew her name—)

& it wasn't because there was a girl playing Justin who smelled like soap & smiled when she flicked bangs from her brunette eyes (I sighed, leaning my head into the basket of her thighs when we claimed a minute, hoping my heartbeat didn't clang its bell)

but because the birthday girl was Britney & each time their hands fluttered like dizzy birds to meet, I swallowed honey, spoke a quiet sweet enough to drown. What did I know about myself that wasn't a key in the wrong lock? This desire, unaffordable—the dusty pocketbook of my heart clamped shut.

Tyler Gillespie

When I Was Straight

i still spoke with crooked letter   crooked letter.
a citrus slice   i slurped words   then said them

short & sweet. of course, saussure argues   an arbitrary

relationship exists   between signifier & sign, so we
can never think   of the same eden twice   while
others say   we can't step foot in the garden anyway.

i'm unsure of my beliefs   on synchronicity, but in this

san serif poem   seraphim snap their wings & rhythm
step as we plant our own stories.   sing our own songs.

J.D. Isip

When I Was Straight

I schooled myself in distance, extracting want
from touch, watching it deoxidize into rust red
and lust left, mostly, clinging to beaker walls,
whist I, I at my arms-length, clung to a rounded
shoulder cap, a bicep, chest, stomach, latching
myself fully to a man I didn't want, could hold
like this, could not want, could bring me to my
need, call it a game, call it a match, call him
every night, to wrestle, to practice, not wanting.

We would enter the laboratory separately, check
our instruments, make sure everything was clean,
washed and pristine, his room made me think
of a butchery, how the interim of slicing and blood
is clinical and white, how there are animals, meat
is different, meat doesn't talk back, doesn't moan
or protest, doesn't have eyes, we always look away,
it's just parts, ribs and haunches, it's what you eat,
when you are hungry for something you haven't had.

Charles Jensen

When I Was Straight

I was transparent—

        —a window boys looked through

    and saw an unpeopled place.

        I was too much—

                  and often, too little—

these lands could not sustain crops

      or love

           or the imagination of desire.

     I knew if only they'd

come close enough—

            they'd see the phantom within me—

They'd see

        a faint reflection—

    They'd see

        themselves.

Ben Kline

When I Was Straight

I stowed twenty twenties / inside my reading copy of *Deadpool* #1 / for any abortions / Andi & me might need / We lost track of her cycles / couldn't tell gibbous from crescent / couldn't afford birth control / or buy condoms / without someone I knew knowing / I was fucking / Didn't matter who / I was already the queer / to the bullies / & cousins / too curious / to come / too close. / Months after the *Casey* decision, we had a scare / The longest two months of my life / The clinic would've made us wait hours / maybe a week / & watch videos / from under our Cobain bangs / Life-saving procedures / as snuff films / Viscous sounds & air / screaming no / but yes / We'd picked Gabriel / but any kid / would be turning 30 now / Fuck / I'd be a grandpa / probably Pawpaw / married at last / to a man / maybe two / Andi under black tar in '97 / We hadn't spoken / since I wasn't straight / to yes / when she asked about marriage / to escape our trailers / near the end of the second month / en route to the multiplex / to watch *The Crying Game* / when she pointed to Wal-Mart / I'd preferred Michael / & she emerged with an open box / of maxi pads / a three-pack / of Hanes / two boxes of Dweebs

Travis Chi Wing Lau

When I Was Straight

I relearned how to walk.

By bearing the crucible
of wetted summers
and the shine of rusting lockers,

slick against my forehead
and tight against my throat
full of my own throbbing,

my body made itself
anew with motion, cruel
with spreading stasis.

And in this remaking was
a deadening, a honeysuckle
trammeled in its silent blooming

beneath cleat and rumor
until malformation became
new nature.

The upright gait of a man
walking away from himself
when it was meant

to meander.

Caridad Moro-Gronlier

When I Was Straight

I married a straight man & stayed
married for sixteen straight years.

I said I love you straight-faced,
but I knew the truth—I was no straight arrow.

My parents thought I held a straight flush
when I brought home a boy with straight blonde hair

& blue eyes, a real straight shooter who asked Papi
if he could take me off his hands. Straightaway,

Papi said yes. I was 20 & it was time to straighten
me up & out of his house. He hoped that straightlaced

Americano would make me walk the straight
& narrow, straitjacket my mouth, & remove

the straight edged razor from my demeanor,
but that boy thought I was straight up awesome

even though I felt straight up awful that I wasn't
straightforward about kissing my best girlfriend

or just how dire the straits of my desire for her
were, a want I was not straightbred for.

For sixteen years I tried, but I was never straight
with him until I walked straight out the door.

Lesléa Newman

When I Was Straight

I studied the girls in the girls room
lined up after lunch before a row
of cold silver sinks as they uncapped gold
tubes of frosted lipstick, swiped
left to right across bottom lip
right to left across top, then rolled
both lips inward before releasing
them with a self-satisfied pink *pop!*
Next each girl as if on cue, leaned
towards the mirror above her sink
but somehow at the same time
backed away to avoid getting her waist
wet while puckering up as if she were
about to kiss her own immaculate reflection.
Sometimes one girl would gently tap
the tip of her right polished pinky
against the southwest corner of her mouth
smoothing an invisible smear which seemed
to be a signal: *ladies, put away your lipstick
and whip out your mascara!*
Now each girl brandished a wand
in the air, like a miniature baton before
raising it to her eyelashes which grew dark
darker, darkest, while I stood on the fringes
waiting to wash my hands, nails bitten
to the quick, not filed into perfect ovals

like these pearly girly girls
or the mother/daughter duo
in that commercial for Jergens lotion
who giggled at how alike they looked:
hair smoothed into bouncy flips,
dresses with sweetheart necklines
cinched at Scarlet O'Hara waists,
Who was the mom? Who was the teen?
They could be sisters as they rubbed creamy
white cream into their hands and then caressed
their own hairless freckle-free forearms
rubbing the slick grease round and round
in synchronized suggestive gestures
while a velvety voice that belonged to a man
waiting in the wings or perhaps to God boomed,
"Even their hands don't give them away."
Oh how my mother longed to give me away
in exchange for a daughter who knew her way
around a makeup bag, a daughter
who wasn't fat, frizzy-haired, and flat-footed,
a daughter who didn't talk
back or favor baggy army pants
over skin tight mini-skirts,
a daughter who knew how to flirt,
who gladly skipped seconds, said no
thank you to dessert,
a daughter who wanted nothing
more than a husband and children
and who didn't dare stare
at the girls in the girls room
so intently that one of them glared
back and asked, "What are you, a lezzie?"
which made all the others shriek
with laughter as they tossed their tools

of the trade back into the unzipped bellies
of their shoulder bags and then marched
back to class single file, leaving me
to my lonesome with all those mirrors
like an un-fun funhouse
reflecting myself back to me,
the only girl in the girls room
hopelessly bent on being straight.

Mel Sherrer

When I Was Straight

I thought I'd act *like a lady*
and like it. What did I know?

I knew about steel and flint,
stone and blade,
how one body can spark
life inside of another—
how one life sharpens the other.

I knew what women could do
alone together in a room—
or alone in this world.

Nicole Tallman

When I Was Straight

I hung the posters of hunks
in my locker and bedroom
alongside red-headed heroines
to avoid questions, to avoid
the truth: I worshipped women.
I hid my lust like a leprous limb.
It greened. I buried it.
A priest detected my stench,
handed me a psalm. It greened.
I buried it in a dusty dresser drawer.
I hung onto hope like my mother,
who said she'd rather I had cancer
than be *that way*. She couldn't bring
herself to say the word gay.
Before my mother died of cancer,
she told me she was proud
of me. I still ask myself:
Does dying bring us closer to acceptance?

Addie Tsai

When I Was Straight

I inhaled your sense of humor,
your long wavy locks the shade
of the bold Texas sun, your flannels

and acid-washed jeans reminiscent
of Darlene, another crush

I wouldn't understand
for a minute yet.

It wasn't all fun & games.
You and Stefannie tricked me,

tied the laces of my sneakers
just before we had to run the 1.5,

and laughed as I fell and scraped
my knees, pride, heart, that fell for you.

Somehow, I still came over, performed
a dance in imitation of *The King & I*,

my favorite, with the Asian fan
I just happened to keep in my backpack

for such an occasion as this one,
to win the attention of my swoon

& bully, all rolled into one
confusing, aching feeling.

The next day, you pretended
we were strangers, yelled

I never liked you in front of Amber,
my favorite cheerleader with ambered

skin, and hair that matched, wiggly
like my favorite caterpillars, or

the little creatures I made
in the cafeteria from straws and milk.

What would have happened if you
disrobed from your flannel of protection,
& wrapped it around us, an invisible cape?

MT Vallarta

When I Was Straight

i picture a dollhouse
i sit with shadows in the middle
crickets bleed outside the window
a tree shaves its own bark
i tiptoe in grasshopper feet
and slip nectar between my
legs   the walls are made of teak
i smell my grandfather's pomade
all bougainvillea and turpentine—
damn   i would turn back
time so i can buy myself
lavender   wipe liquid crystal
off my eyes   pierce a moon
in my nostril   trill my most
damnest self into
symphony   i will never die
again thinking *god*
i'm so glad
it's over

Julie Marie Wade

When I Was Straight

I did not love women as I do now.
I loved them with my eyes closed, my back turned.
I loved them silent & startled & shy.

The world was a dreamless slumber party,
sleeping bags like straitjackets spread out on
the living room floor, my face pressed into a

slender pillow.

All night I woke to rain on the strangers' windows.
No one remembered to leave a light on in the hall.
Someone's father seemed always to be shaving.

When I stood up, I tried to tiptoe
around the sleeping bodies, their long hair
speckled with confetti, their faces blanched by the

porch-light moon.

I never knew exactly where the bathroom was.
I tried to wake the host girl to ask her, but she was
only one adrift in that sea of bodies. I was ashamed

to say they all looked the same to me, beautiful &
untouchable as stars. It would be years before
I learned to find anyone in the sumptuous,

terrifying dark.

Afterword

I can't remember a time when I was straight and I can't remember a time I was not queer lesbian, gay, bi, or a gendered he or she, him or her, or mostly somewhere in between. Nor do I remember a time when Maureen was straight.

Neither of us knew each other in that before time, enacting what was expected of us, trying to ignore what our bodies and souls were telling us about desire. What I do remember is Maureen, early in our friendship, sitting on my fold-up futon bed in my tiny apartment on 10th Street in New York's East Village. The living room was the bedroom in that apartment. Next to the bedroom/living room was a center room that was both kitchen and bathroom, the tub next to the one small sink, a cramped toilet closet in the corner. There was one other room, a windowless cell, maybe 8' x 8', that held my books and a small desk, on which sat an electric typewriter and a notebook. Maureen and I spent many hours talking in that apartment, sharing the beginnings of, for both of us, what was to become a writing life.

One thing was clear—Maureen and I were not straight. How we weren't straight wasn't quite as clear, although then we both identified strongly as lesbian, often working out our desire on the page until it became a reality in our lives. Although we were very different kinds of writers, I always understood Maureen as a fellow traveler, both of us more comfortable as seekers willing to let our work and desire be the guides we followed to self-knowledge and unknown destinations.

When we began to write together, many years after we first met, we both understood how our differences often served and ignited our collaborations. Maureen and I were never lovers, but the work we did together was deeply honest, as it must be in the most intimate of relationships, filled with love, play, flow, humor, trust, impatience, hesitation, merging, pushing away, then merging again, never static or fixed. Flirtation, games, anger, jokes, fear, desire, harmony—it was all there and more.

Maureen inspired the same in almost everyone she met. In this gorgeous tribute volume of poems, I feel her spirit, her exquisite ability to look at herself in her poems with humility, humor, and honesty. The poets here trust the writing to reflect the body's desire as it leads one past all efforts to fulfill what is expected. The alternative of course is a spiritual numbness, always a kind of death. Maureen understood this, and even in her passing, she continues to inspire and teach us how we might live.

Samuel Ace
October, 2024

An excerpt from Portals *by Maureen Seaton and Samuel Ace*

Lunes

Think of me
Lashed foreign in your arms—
The brutal feminine.

I'm afraid
the breasts
have flattened
into the wind
foremost
on the ship
head carved
boyish   brutal
and sudden
given to the horse
rushing away
through the field

My dog took
me down
that same path
more solid
than the wailing chest

Think of me
open and digital, a sound
exhaled in G.

Aching   a revival
of paint   a wooden
hush in the feral quiet

A zero blue
frozen and linked, pushed back
to the elegy.

I do
think of you
all the time
as if seeing
would manifest
you here
not irrevocably lost

Nor borrowed (from
fire), from the red book
of thirty-four children.

Fight me
for a ranch
to put them
bunks
but wait
you said paint
not souls

Yet here I
am alive in the frayed
and fragile past.

The Extraordinary Maureen Seaton

Maureen Seaton (she/her), an adored Mama and Grammy, celebrated writer, beloved creative writing teacher, and all-around magical person, died peacefully on August 26, 2023 at the age of 75 in Longmont, CO. Throughout her 6+ year journey with cancer, she remained positive and connected to life. She continued to write both independently and collaboratively, attended her Friday poetry group of Tres Abuelas y Una Mama, spent time basking in the light of her one and only grandson Mikey, and took countless walks with her dog Binky, her friend Linda, and her daughters Emily and Jennifer. She continued to adore the natural world, laugh her heart out with Lori every night, and dance to loud music in the car. Every day in hospice care, often while eating a pint of her favorite pistachio coconut ice cream for lunch and laughing with a loved one under the linden tree, she commented that "life is good," and she meant it.

Maureen Seaton, a proud libra, was born on October 20, 1947, in Elizabeth, NJ to Frank and Joan Seaton. She is preceded in death by her parents and her brother Frank Seaton Jr. She is survived by her partner Lori Anderson, her daughters Jennifer Steele and Emily Blank, her sons-in-law Andrew Steele and Matthew Blank, her grandson Mikey Blank, her sister Melissa Koons, and her beloved dog Binky.

Maureen grew up in New Jersey and Long Island. In high school she excelled at English, piano, and religion. She planned to become a nun until she met her first husband and started a family. Until 1992, along the Hudson River (where she felt most at home) Maureen raised two daughters, got sober, began writing poetry, and met her life-partner Lori. Her favorite pizza was Ray's Original broccoli and ricotta, but she was known to grab some Two Boots in the village after a late night of dancing with Jennie.

Maureen moved with her family from New York to Chicago in 1992 and launched her writing and teaching career. She taught poetry workshops and served as Artist-in-Residence at Columbia College Chicago from 1993–2002, teaching concurrently in the MFA in Creative Writing program at the School of the Art Institute of Chicago from 1997–1999. She received her MFA in Creative Writing/Poetry from Vermont College of Fine Arts in 1996. In 2002 she joined the faculty in creative writing at the University of Miami and stayed there until she retired in 2020. Maureen loved teaching and her students.

Maureen authored more than two dozen books of poetry and one memoir. Some of her solo books of poetry include *Fear of Subways* (1991), winner of the Eighth Mountain Poetry Prize; *Furious Cooking* (1996), winner of both the Iowa Poetry Prize and a Lambda Literary Award; *Venus Examines Her Breast* (2004), winner of the Publishing Triangle's Audre Lorde Award; *Cave of the Yellow Volkswagen* (2009); *Fibonacci Batman: New and Selected Poems* (2013); *Undersea* (2021); *Fisher* (2018); *Sweet World* (2019), first place winner of the Florida Book Award; and *The Sky is an Elephant* (2023). Her memoir *Sex Talks to Girls* (2008 and reissued 2018) earned her a second Lambda Literary Award.

In addition to her solo work, Maureen also was a prolific, energetic, and generous collaborator. She wrote with and published several collaborative books with Denise Duhamel, Samuel Ace, Neil de la Flor, Aaron Smith, Kristine Snodgrass, Nicole Tallman, Carolina Hospital, Nicole Hospital-Medina, and Holly Iglesias. Maureen's work was read widely and received many accolades. In addition to her "lammy" awards, she was the recipient of a National Endowment for the Arts Fellowship and a grant from the Illinois Arts Council. Her poems appear in issues of *The Best American Poetry* and the *Pushcart Prize: Best of the Small Presses*. She was voted "Miami's Best Poet" in 2020 by *The Miami New Times*.

At home, Maureen was the matriarch of her small family which also included many "adopted" friends who were like family. She hosted New Moon Circles, Winter Solstice Rituals, and family brunches. She taught us the names of her favorite trees and birds. Yet mostly the family simply gathered, sharing from the heart, supporting each other through all of life's ups and downs, laughing even during the darkest times, and simply enjoying being together. The birth of her grandson in 2013 was of course a highlight for her and for many years she and Mikey (Sebby back then) enjoyed a weekly "Grammy and Sebby day of fun!"

Whether you were her sister, daughter, partner, friend, son-in-law, grandson, niece, nephew, collaborator, or student, Maureen believed in you and loved you so unconditionally that you couldn't help but want to strive to heal and love yourself, embrace your dreams, and rise to the creative occasion with courage.

—Maureen's obituary published on September 11, 2023.

Acknowledgements

Kelli Russell Agodon. "When I Was Straight." Copyright © 2023 by Kelli Russell Agodon. First published in *Limp Wrist*. Reprinted by permission of the author.

Allison Blevins. "When I Was Straight." Copyright © 2023 by Allison Blevins. First published in *Limp Wrist*. Reprinted by permission of the author.

Emma Bolden. "When I Was Straight." Copyright © 2023 by Emma Bolden. First published in *Limp Wrist*. Reprinted by permission of the author.

Dustin Brookshire. "When I Was Straight." Copyright © 2023 by Dustin Brookshire. First published in *TAB Journal*. Reprinted by permission of the author.

J.D. Isip. "When I Was Straight." Copyright © 2023 by J.D. Isip. First published in *Limp Wrist*. Reprinted by permission of the author.

Caridad Moro-Gronlier. "When I Was Straight." Copyright © 2023 by Caridad Moro-Gronlier. First published in *Pleaides*. Reprinted by permission of the author.

Lesléa Newman. "When I Was Straight." Copyright © 2023 by Lesléa

Newman. First published as "Hellbent in High School, 1973" in *Pangyrus*. Reprinted by permission of the author.

Maureen Seaton. "When I Was Straight." Copyright © 2001 by Maureen Seaton. Published in *Little Ice Age* (Invisible City Press, 2001). Reprinted by permission of the author's estate.

Julie Marie Wade. "When I Was Straight." Copyright © 2014 by Julie Marie Wade. Published as "When I Was Straight [I did not love women]" in *When I Was Straight* (A Midsummer Night's Press, 2014). Reprinted by permission of the author.

Bios

Kelli Russell Agodon (she/her) is a bi/queer poet, writer, and editor from the Pacific Northwest. Her newest books are *Dialogues with Rising Tides* (Copper Canyon Press), which was named a Finalist in the Washington State Book Awards and *Demystifying the Manuscript: Essays and Interviews on Creating a Book of Poems* coedited with Susan Rich. She is the cofounder of Two Sylvias Press and teaches at Pacific Lutheran University's low-res MFA program, the Rainier Writing Workshop. Kelli is the cohost of the poetry series "Poems You Need" with Melissa Studdard. agodon.com / twosylviaspress.com / youtube.com/@PoemsYouNeed

Clayre Benzadón (she/her) is a queer (bi /pan) Sephardic (Mizrahi)-Askhenazi poet, educator (adjunct professor) and activist. Her chapbook, *Liminal Zenith*, was published by SurVision Books in 2019. Her manuscript, *Moon as Salted Lemon* was recently named an honorable mention for Miami Book Fair's 2025 Emerging Writer's Fellowship and was chosen as a winner for Driftwood Press's Editor's Pick Poetry Prize. Find more about her here: clayrebenzadon.com.

Allison Blevins (she/her) is a queer disabled writer and the author of *Where Will We Live if the House Burns Down?*, *Cataloguing Pain*, *Handbook for the Newly Disabled: A Lyric Memoir*, *Slowly/Suddenly*, and five chapbooks. Winner of the 2023 Lexi Rudnitsky Editor's Choice Award from Persea Books and the 2022 Laux/Millar Poetry Prize from *Raleigh Review*, Allison serves as the Publisher of Small Harbor Publishing. She lives in Minnesota with her spouse and three children. allisonblevins.com

Emma Bolden (she/her) is the author of a memoir, *The Tiger and the Cage* (Soft Skull), and the poetry collections *House Is an Enigma, medi(t)ations*, and *Maleficae*. Her work has appeared in such journals as the *Gettysburg Review*, the *Mississippi Review*, *The Rumpus*, *StoryQuarterly*, *Prairie Schooner*, *New Madrid*, *TriQuarterly*, *Shenandoah*, *Ploughshares*, and *Pleiades*. The recipient of an NEA Fellowship, she is an editor of *Screen Door Review: Literary Voices of the Queer South*.

Regie Cabico (he/she/they) is the first openly queer and Asian American Poet to win the Nuyorican Poets Cafe Grand Slam and took top prizes in 3 National Poetry Slams and appeared on HBO, MTV, and TEDx Talk and is featured in two episodes of The Poet Speaks on The Archeology Channel. Cabico is the author of *A Rabbit In Search of a Rolex* published by Day Eight.

Sarah Cooper is a Canadian-American academic and currently, a Visiting Assistant Professor in the English Department at Colorado State University. Her interdisciplinary research resides at the intersection of archives, rhetoric, gender and queer theory, and sexuality studies. Most recently, her research appears in the *Journal of Lesbian Studies*. She is also the author of two poetry collections: *Permanent Marker* (Paper Nautilus, 2020) and *89%* (Clemson University Press, 2022).

James Davis (he/him) is the author of *Club Q*, which won the Anthony Hecht Poetry Prize. His poems have been featured on NBC News and CBC Radio and anthologized in *Best New Poets 2011* and *2019*. Other publication credits include poems and essays in *The Sewanee Review*, *The Gettysburg Review, Copper Nickel, Bennington Review, DIAGRAM*, and many other notable venues. He holds a PhD in English from the University of North Texas, where he teaches writing. His website is jamesdavispoet.com.

Theresa Davis (she/her) is the author of *After This We Go Dark* and *Drowned: A Mermaid's Manifesto* (Sibling Rivalry Press, 2016). She is a multifaceted artist and educator who has made a significant impact on the world of poetry, education, and storytelling. An acclaimed poet, storyteller, educator, and author, Theresa is known for her dynamic presence both on stage and in the classroom.

Aaron DeLee (he/him) received his MFA from Northwestern University and has work published in places such as *Assaracus, Court Green, Limp Wrist,* and *Rougarou.* He teaches the occasional poetry workshop at the Leather Archives & Museum in Chicago. Besides poetry, he also practices sumi-e painting and calligraphy through the Japanese Culture Center.

Diamond Forde (she/her) is the author of *Mother Body*, a 2022 Kate Tufts Discovery award finalist and the forthcoming *Book of Alice* (Scribner, 2026). Her work has appeared in *Poetry Magazine, Ninth Letter, Tupelo Quarterly,* and more. You can find out more at her website: diamondforde.com.

Tyler Gillespie (he/him) is the author of the nonfiction collection *The Thing about Florida: Exploring a Misunderstood State* (University Press of Florida, 2021) and two poetry collections—*the nature machine!* (Autofocus, 2023) and *Florida Man: Poems, Revisited* (Burrow Press, 2024). Instagram: tyler_gills

J.D. Isip (he/him) is the author of the full-length poetry collections *Kissing the Wound* (Moon Tide Press, 2023) and *Pocketing Feathers* (Sadie Girl Press, 2015). His third collection, *Reluctant Prophets*, will be released by Moon Tide Press in early 2025. J.D. lives in Texas with his dogs, Ivy and Bucky.

Charles Jensen (he/him) wrote *Splice of Life: A Memoir in 13 Film Genres*. His most recent collection of poetry is *Instructions between Take-*

off and Landing. His previous books include two collections of poetry and seven chapbooks of cross-genre work. The City of Los Angeles Department of Cultural Affairs designated him a 2019–2020 Cultural Trailblazer. His poetry has appeared in *American Poetry Review, Crab Orchard Review, The Journal, New England Review,* and *Prairie Schooner*, and essays have appeared in *Exposition Review, The Florida Review, The Los Angeles Times,* and *Passages North*.

Ben Kline (he/him) lives in Cincinnati, Ohio. A poet, storyteller and Madonna mega-fan slash podcaster, as well as a co-coordinator and MC of Poetry Stacked at the University of Cincinnati, Ben is the author of the chapbooks *Sagittarius A** and *Dead Uncles*, as well as the full-length collections *It Was Never Supposed to Be* (Variant Literature) and *Twang* (ELJ Editions.) His work has appeared in *Poet Lore, Copper Nickel, Florida Review, Southeast Review, DIAGRAM, Poetry*, and other publications. You can find, learn, and read more at linktr.ee/benkline.

Travis Chi Wing Lau (he/him/his) is Assistant Professor of English at Kenyon College. His research and teaching focus on eighteenth- and nineteenth-century British literature and culture, health humanities, and disability studies. Alongside his scholarship, Lau frequently writes for venues of public scholarship like *Synapsis: A Journal of Health Humanities, Public Books, Lapham's Quarterly*, and *The Los Angeles Review of Books*. His poetry has appeared in *Wordgathering, Glass, South Carolina Review, Foglifter*, and *Hypertext*, as well as in three chapbooks, *The Bone Setter* (Damaged Goods Press, 2019), *Paring* (Finishing Line Press, 2020), and *Vagaries* (Fork Tine Press, 2022). travisclau.com

Caridad Moro-Gronlier (she/her) is the Poet Laureate of Miami-Dade County. She is the author of *Tortillera* (TRP, 2021), *Visionware*, (FLP, 2009) and the recipient of the 2023 Julia Peterkin Literary Award. She is the editor of *Grabbed: Poets and Writers Respond to Sexual Assault, Empowerment and Healing* (Beacon Press, 2020) and associate editor for *SWWIM Every Day*, as well as the Poetry Curator-At-Large for The

Betsy Hotel. Recent work can be found or is forthcoming from *Essential Queer Voices of U.S. Poetry*, *MER*, *The Power of the Feminine I*, *Under a Warm Green Linden*, *The Blue Mountain Review*, and others. She lives in Miami, FL with her wife and son.

Lesléa Newman (she/her) has created 86 books for readers of all ages including the dual memoir-in-verse, *I Carry My Mother* and *I Wish My Father*; the novel-in-verse, *October Mourning: A Song for Matthew Shepard*, and the book-length fully-illustrated biographical poem, *Always Matt: A Tribute to Matthew Shepard*. She has also published many children's books including *Sparkle Boy*; *The Boy Who Cried Fabulous*; and *Heather Has Two Mommies*. Her literary awards include a poetry fellowship from the National Endowment for the Arts, two National Jewish Book Awards, and two Stonewall Honors. From 2008–2010, she served as the poet laureate of Northampton, MA. lesleanewman.com

Mel Sherrer (she/her) is a poet and performer from Las Vegas, Nevada. She received her B.F.A. from Hollins University in Roanoke, Virginia, and her M.F.A. in Poetry from Converse University in Spartanburg, South Carolina. She currently teaches courses in Performance Literature and Poetry and serves as the Associate Editor for *Sage Cigarettes Magazine*. Find her work and more information at MelSherrer.com.

Nicole Tallman (she/her) is the author of four collections: *Something Kindred*, *Poems for the People*, *FERSACE*, and *Julie, or Sylvia*. She serves as Miami's official Poetry Ambassador, Editor of Redacted Books, and Poetry Editor for *South Florida Poetry Journal* and *The Blue Mountain Review*. Find her on social media @natallman and at nicoletallman.com.

A biracial Asian artist and writer, **Addie Tsai** (any/all) teaches at William & Mary. Addie collaborated with Dominic Walsh Dance Theater on *Victor Frankenstein* and *Camille Claudel*, among others. They are the author of *Dear Twin* and *Unwieldy Creatures*, which was a Shirley Jackson finalist for Best Novel. She is the features & reviews editor, as well as fiction co-editor, for *Anomaly*, and the founding editor in chief for *just femme & dandy*. More at addietsai.com.

MT Vallarta (they/them) is the author of the poetry collection, *What You Refuse to Remember*, winner of the 2022 Small Harbor Publishing Laureate Prize. They have received awards and fellowships from the Martha's Vineyard Institute of Creative Writing, Roots. Wounds. Words., The Rowan Foundation, and others. Their work can be found in *The Selkie*, *Shō*, *Madwoman in the Attic*, *Nat. Brut*, and elsewhere. Currently, they are an Assistant Professor of Ethnic Studies at California Polytechnic State University, San Luis Obispo.

Julie Marie Wade (she/her) writes and publishes poetry, prose, and hybrid forms, most recently *Fugue: An Aural History* (Diagram/New Michigan Press, 2023) and *Otherwise: Essays* (Autumn House, 2023). Her forthcoming collections include *The Mary Years* (Texas Review Press, 2024), selected by Michael Martone for the 2023 Clay Reynolds Novella Prize, and *Quick Change Artist: Poems* (Anhinga Press, 2025), selected by Octavio Quintanilla for the 2023 Anhinga Prize in Poetry. Wade teaches in the creative writing program at Florida International University in Miami and makes her home with Angie Griffin and their two cats in Dania Beach. juliemariewade.com

About the Editor

Dustin Brookshire (he/him) is the author of the forthcoming chapbook *Repeat As Needed* (Harbor Editions, 2025) and the chapbooks *Never Picked First For Playtime* (Harbor Editions, 2023), *Love Most Of You Too* (Harbor Editions, 2021) and *To The One Who Raped Me* (Sibling Rivalry Press, 2012). *Love Most Of You Too* and *Never Picked First For Playtime* were finalists in the Poetry Chapbook category of the American Book Fest's Best Book Awards in 2022 and 2023, respectively.

Along with poet Julie E. Bloemeke, Dustin is the co-editor of *Let Me Say This: A Dolly Parton Poetry Anthology* (Madville Publishing, 2023). In 2024, *Let Me Say This* was awarded a Nautilus silver medal and named to the "Books All Georgians Should Read" list by the Georgia Center for the Book. In 2023, *Let Me Say This* was a finalist in the Poetry Anthologies category of the American Book Fest's Best Book Awards. *The Slowdown*, episodes 1109 and 1139, featured poems from *Let Me Say This*. In September 2024, *Let Me Say This* inspired the Poetry Well production *Let Me Say This: A Dolly Parton Tribute Concert* at Joe's Pub.

Dustin is recipient of the 2024 Jon Tribble Editors Fellowship at Poetry by the Sea and a runner up in the 2024 Desert Rat Residency Poetry Contest. In 2021, he was a finalist for the Key West Literary

Seminar's Scotti Merrill Award. Dustin has been twice nominated for the Best of the Net and Pushcart Prize. In 2023, his work was featured in Georgia Poetry in the Parks.

Dustin's poetry has been published in numerous journals, and he's been anthologized in *Divining Divas: 100 Gay Men on their Muses* (Lethe Press, 2012), *The Queer South: LGBTQ Writes on the American South* (Sibling Rivalry Press, 2014), *Braving the Body* (Harbor Anthologies, 2024), and *Invisible Strings: 113 Poets respond to the songs of Taylor Swift* (Ballantine Books, 2024).

More at dustinbrookshire.com.

About Small Harbor Publishing

Small Harbor Publishing is a 501c3 nonprofit organization. Our goal is to publish unique and diverse voices. We are a feminist press, and we are committed to diversity and inclusion. We strive to fiercely promote the work of our authors and to bring new voices to a devoted and expanding readership.

Small Harbor Publishing began in 2018 with the first issue of *Harbor Review*. The magazine is an online space where poetry and art converse. *Harbor Review* quickly grew and now publishes reviews and runs three micro chapbook competitions, the Washburn Prize, the Editor's Prize, and the Jewish American Woman's Prize.

In July 2020, Small Harbor Publishing was officially incorporated and began Harbor Editions. Harbor Editions accepts submissions through a chapbook open reading period, a hybrid chapbook open reading period, the Marginalia Series, and the Laureate Prize.

In 2023, Harbor Anthologies began with a mission to promote texts that explore social justice issues and highlight marginalized writers.

If you would like to support Small Harbor Publishing, please visit our "About" page at smallharborpublishing.com/about.

Maureen

Made in the USA
Columbia, SC
06 January 2025